KITTY KOANS

ZEN MUSINGS OF
THE DALI CLAWMA

DALI CLAWMA

"Kitty Koans: Zen Musings of the Dali Clawma" is a profound collection of haiku poems that embody the timeless wisdom of Zen philosophy. Through feline eyes, we are invited to see the world with fresh clarity and a sense of wonder. With whimsical and surreal imagery, these poems explore themes of nature, love, enlightenment, curiosity, laziness, and the fickle nature of cats. From their high perch, they watch the world go by, and in their plentiful down-time, they ponder the mysteries of existence. This book is for the spiritual seeker who wants to deepen their bond with their feline friend and understand the inner workings of their cat's mind.

TABLE OF CONTENTS

CHAPTER 1

The Zen Cat Ponders

With a graceful leap,
I am free from all burdens,
Zen cat in motion.

Eyes open or closed,
I am present in this meow.
Zen cat, here and now.

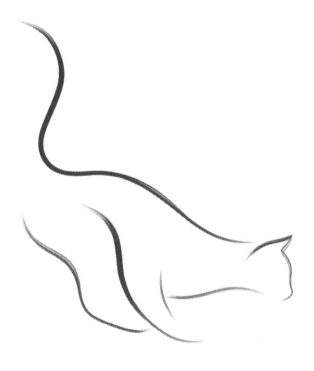

On the countertop,
a Zen cat watches and waits
easy prey spotted.

The sound of the wind:
a soothing symphony plays.
Zen cat listens on.

Life's impermanence
a Zen cat's gift of insight:
Savor each moment.

In the deep darkness,
my eyes shine like stars above;
Zen cat's inner light.

Zen cat rests with ease:
whether donut or loaf, the
mind and body still.

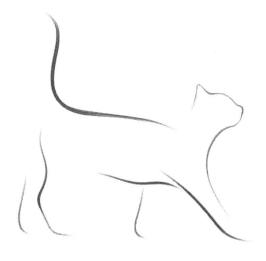

With each passing breath,
I am closer to the truth:
A Zen cat's journey.

In the garden's calm,
butterflies dance, flowers sway,
Zen cat watches all.

From his vantage point,
the Zen cat sees life's drama
free from attachment.

The mind's wild chatter
quiets to a gentle hum
in the Zen cat's realm.

A flower in bloom
nature's perfect masterpiece
a Zen cat's wonder.

From his lofty perch,
the Zen cat surveys the world
And passes judgement.

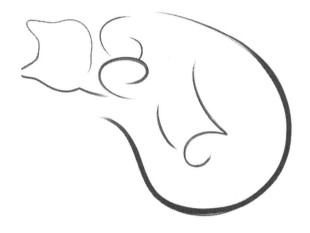

In the morning light,
nature's beauty awakens;
a Zen cat's delight.

Watching from on high,
the Zen cat sees life unfold:
A moment in time.

A feline's movements,
graceful and full of beauty
Zen cat's truest form.

CHAPTER 2

Waking to the World Anew

The world rushes by.
I am still, watching it all.
Silent, steady, calm.

Stretching in the sun,
my muscles loose, my heart light,
breathing in pure bliss.

In nature's embrace,
at one with the universe.
A cat's Zen within.

Basking in the sun,
a cat's fur warmed by its rays:
pure bliss, no worries.

In the morning mist,
a four-legged Zen master
contemplates the world.

In the heart of night
the cat sleeps, but his spirit
roams through starry skies.

Lithe body, so sleek.
A feline form in motion;
beauty, grace, and poise.

Can opener hums,
a Zen cat's ears perk up quick.
Hope for Fancy Feast.

CHAPTER 3

In Meditation

The mouse scurries by.
I watch, but do not pursue.
Content with what is.

Whiskers twitch, eyes close.
In meditation I find
true timeless pleasure.

In the stillness, I
am a feline work of art.
Perfectly serene.

How to be content?
With each day I find more peace
in this simple life.

In the sunlight's warmth,
I find solace and comfort.
Cat meditation.

Soft steps on the floor,
cat's mobile meditation.
Grace in every move.

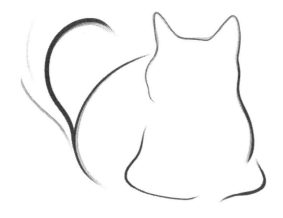

A cat's tail sways like
A pendulum in motion,
hypnotic and calm.

CHAPTER 4

Wonders of Nature

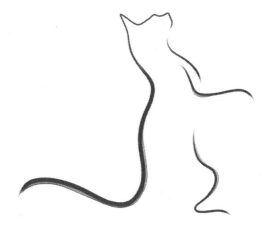

With each step I take
I feel the earth's soft embrace;
nature's gentle flow.

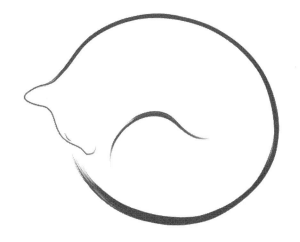

On a rainy day,
the cat seeks shelter, curled up.
A warm, dry, Zen loaf.

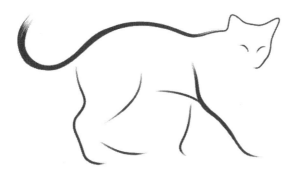

Soft paws on the ground
graceful steps, a feline dance
beauty in motion.

In the autumn breeze
leaves rustle, dance in the air:
a Zen state of mind.

Fleeting thoughts and dreams:
ephemeral like the breeze.
Cat's truth in motion.

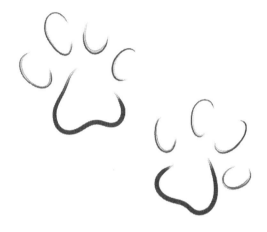

In the winter snow,
a paw print marks the stillness:
Zen's purest form found.

Petals softly fall.
Life's transience in motion.
A master cat smiles.

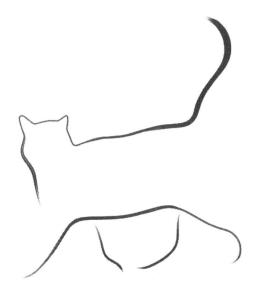

A feline's swift grace:
slender body in motion,
beauty unsurpassed.

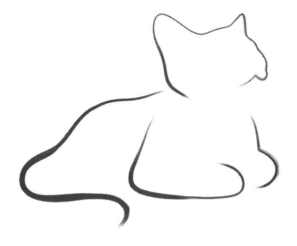

The whispering wind,
nature's gentle breath of life;
a passed cat at peace.

Cherry blossoms dance
in the breeze of life's sweet song.
The Zen heart abides.

CHAPTER 5

Curiosity and Play

In a single leap
I attain enlightenment:
a moment of truth.

Curiosity:
exploring the unknown path,
new mysteries to see.

The Zen cat surveys,
and with a swift paw, he knocks.
Stillness turned chaos.

A feline diva,
graceful and demanding ways;
attention now please.

A fragile vase falls,
beautiful chaos ensues.
Time to make a mess!

Feline obsession
laser pointer shining bright.
Joy, pure and simple.

From the counter top,
a Zen cat smacks with delight
your favorite mug.

Houseplants in my sight,
a truly delightful feast,
Nature's sweetest treats.

Kitty Koans

Knocking things around.
Delightful flurry of paws.
Feline chaos reigns.

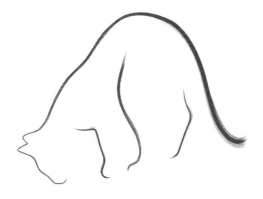

Nine lives to explore,
a cat's curiosity:
dimensions unknown.

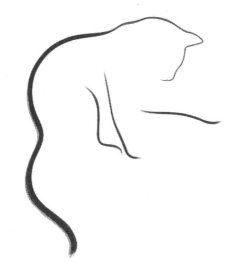

Toppled book or vase,
household order overturned;
Zen's playful nature.

Feline Picasso:
paw prints pressed on your clean work,
museum crowds awe-struck.

Cat eyes watch it fall
nature's swift experiment
playful Zen mischief.

CHAPTER 6

A Hidden Fierceness

A lap to curl up,
purring with contentment 'til
a paw's sudden swipe.

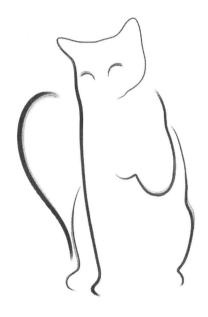

A paw brushes by.
a fleeting touch, but enough
To awaken Zen.

Soft purrs and head rubs,
love and affection abound.
Then claws, teeth, and hiss.

A mouse in his paws!
Life's greatest hunt, Zen's delight
nature's perfect feast.

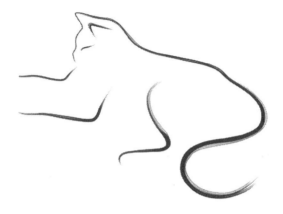

Fickle as can be
a feline heart full of love,
But claws always there.

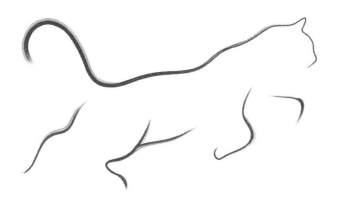

A bird on the wing,
the ultimate, fatal dance.
In a flash, success!

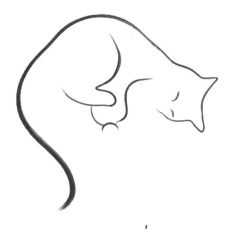

Claws of destruction,
a feline's path of chaos,
objects left in shreds.

Feline paradox:
lap cat, hunter, Zen master
infinite mystery.

CHAPTER 7

Restfulness at Last

Zen thoughts fill my mind,
purring on my human's lap,
peacefully content.

A cat's purring song
echoes through the tranquil room;
a mantra of peace.

A gentle head bump
a Zen cat's love on display
is true affection.

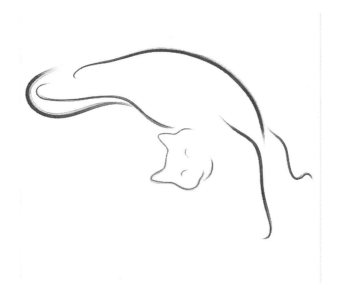

Stretching out so long,
Zen cat's last movement before
rest: the path to peace.

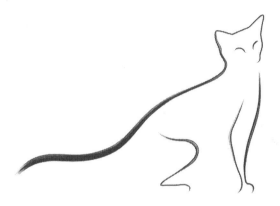

The sound of my purr
echoes through the empty space;
soothing lullaby.

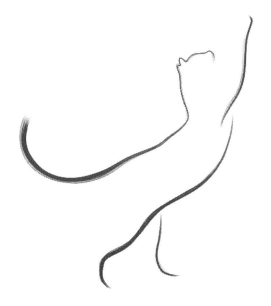

With a stretch and yawn,
a Zen cat seeks peace and calm.
Laziness, the way.

Feline's love so true
purring in my owner's lap
content in my soul.

Made in United States
Orlando, FL
05 November 2024